2020-2021 Homeschool Pl

& RECORD BOOK

THIS PLANNER BELONGS TO

_____ **TO** _____
DATE   DATE

STUDENT   **GRADE**

_____   _____

This **2020-2021 Homeschool Planner** is designed to help you organize the curriculum and records for your student. It accommodates two semesters beginning **August of 2020 through July of 2021 PLUS a bonus month of August 2021**. Set goals and stay on track with weekly, monthly, and yearly planning prompts.

Make lesson plans and document the progress of your child by tracking subjects, assignments, projects, videos watched, grades, attendance, and more. You can list your important contacts, your accounts, passwords, and the field trips/activities you are planning for the year. The monthly calendars have the US Federal Holiday & Observances already populated, There is ample space for notes at the end of each week, month, and semester. At the end of the year, you can reflect and make plans for next year.

Homeschooling is a serious and honorable endeavor. This planner is designed to help you succeed as you educate your child and prepare them for success.

Table of Contents

Contacts

NAME	CONTACT INFORMATION

Account TRACKER

ACCOUNT NAME	PURCHASED DATE	EXPIRE/ RENEWAL	PRICE

Password TRACKER

WEBSITE/ACCOUNT	USERNAME/ LOGIN	PASSWORD

Event TRACKER

SEMESTER 1

FIELD TRIP/ACTIVITIES	DATE	TIME	FEE

SEMESTER 2

FIELD TRIP/ACTIVITIES	DATE	TIME	FEE

NOTES

Yearly SUBJECT Planner

SUBJECT	GOAL	REQUIRED RESOURCE

Yearly **CURRICULUM** *Planner*

BUDGET

SUBJECT	CURRICULUM/SUPPLIES	COST

TOTAL

Our Year At A Glance

IMPORTANT DATES

	AUGUST
	SEPTEMBER
	OCTOBER
	NOVEMBER
	DECEMBER
	JANUARY

	GOAL	ACHIEVED
# OF WEEKS	_____	# OF WEEKS _____
# OF DAYS	_____	# OF DAYS _____

Our Year At A Glance

FEBRUARY

MARCH

APRIL

MAY

JUNE

JULY

GOAL	ACHIEVED
# OF WEEKS _____	# OF WEEKS _____
# OF DAYS _____	# OF DAYS _____

2020 AT A GLANCE

JANUARY 2020
S	M	T	W	T	F	S
			1	2	3	4
5	6	7	8	9	10	11
12	13	14	15	16	17	18
19	20	21	22	23	24	25
26	27	28	29	30	31	

FEBRUARY 2020
S	M	T	W	T	F	S
						1
2	3	4	5	6	7	8
9	10	11	12	13	14	15
16	17	18	19	20	21	22
23	24	25	26	27	28	29

MARCH 2020
S	M	T	W	T	F	S
1	2	3	4	5	6	7
8	9	10	11	12	13	14
15	16	17	18	19	20	21
22	23	24	25	26	27	28
29	30	31				

APRIL 2020
S	M	T	W	T	F	S
			1	2	3	4
5	6	7	8	9	10	11
12	13	14	15	16	17	18
19	20	21	22	23	24	25
26	27	28	29	30		

MAY 2020
S	M	T	W	T	F	S
					1	2
3	4	5	6	7	8	9
10	11	12	13	14	15	16
17	18	19	20	21	22	23
24	25	26	27	28	29	30
31						

JUNE 2020
S	M	T	W	T	F	S
	1	2	3	4	5	6
7	8	9	10	11	12	13
14	15	16	17	18	19	20
21	22	23	24	25	26	27
28	29	30				

JULY 2020
S	M	T	W	T	F	S
			1	2	3	4
5	6	7	8	9	10	11
12	13	14	15	16	17	18
19	20	21	22	23	24	25
26	27	28	29	30	31	

AUGUST 2020
S	M	T	W	T	F	S
						1
2	3	4	5	6	7	8
9	10	11	12	13	14	15
16	17	18	19	20	21	22
23	24	25	26	27	28	29
30	31					

SEPTEMBER 2020
S	M	T	W	T	F	S
		1	2	3	4	5
6	7	8	9	10	11	12
13	14	15	16	17	18	19
20	21	22	23	24	25	26
27	28	29	30			

OCTOBER 2020
S	M	T	W	T	F	S
				1	2	3
4	5	6	7	8	9	10
11	12	13	14	15	16	17
18	19	20	21	22	23	24
25	26	27	28	29	30	31

NOVEMBER 2020
S	M	T	W	T	F	S
1	2	3	4	5	6	7
8	9	10	11	12	13	14
15	16	17	18	19	20	21
22	23	24	25	26	27	28
29	30					

DECEMBER 2020
S	M	T	W	T	F	S
		1	2	3	4	5
6	7	8	9	10	11	12
13	14	15	16	17	18	19
20	21	22	23	24	25	26
27	28	29	30	31		

2021 AT A GLANCE

JANUARY 2021

S	M	T	W	T	F	S
					1	2
3	4	5	6	7	8	9
10	11	12	13	14	15	16
17	18	19	20	21	22	23
24	25	26	27	28	29	30
31						

FEBRUARY 2021

S	M	T	W	T	F	S
	1	2	3	4	5	6
7	8	9	10	11	12	13
14	15	16	17	18	19	20
21	22	23	24	25	26	27
28						

MARCH 2021

S	M	T	W	T	F	S
	1	2	3	4	5	6
7	8	9	10	11	12	13
14	15	16	17	18	19	20
21	22	23	24	25	26	27
28	29	30	31			

APRIL 2021

S	M	T	W	T	F	S
				1	2	3
4	5	6	7	8	9	10
11	12	13	14	15	16	17
18	19	20	21	22	23	24
25	26	27	28	29	30	

MAY 2021

S	M	T	W	T	F	S
						1
2	3	4	5	6	7	8
9	10	11	12	13	14	15
16	17	18	19	20	21	22
23	24	25	26	27	28	29
30	31					

JUNE 2021

S	M	T	W	T	F	S
		1	2	3	4	5
6	7	8	9	10	11	12
13	14	15	16	17	18	19
20	21	22	23	24	25	26
27	28	29	30			

JULY 2021

S	M	T	W	T	F	S
				1	2	3
4	5	6	7	8	9	10
11	12	13	14	15	16	17
18	19	20	21	22	23	24
25	26	27	28	29	30	31

AUGUST 2021

S	M	T	W	T	F	S
1	2	3	4	5	6	7
8	9	10	11	12	13	14
15	16	17	18	19	20	21
22	23	24	25	26	27	28
29	30	31				

SEPTEMBER 2021

S	M	T	W	T	F	S
			1	2	3	4
5	6	7	8	9	10	11
12	13	14	15	16	17	18
19	20	21	22	23	24	25
26	27	28	29	30		

OCTOBER 2021

S	M	T	W	T	F	S
					1	2
3	4	5	6	7	8	9
10	11	12	13	14	15	16
17	18	19	20	21	22	23
24	25	26	27	28	29	30
31						

NOVEMBER 2021

S	M	T	W	T	F	S
	1	2	3	4	5	6
7	8	9	10	11	12	13
14	15	16	17	18	19	20
21	22	23	24	25	26	27
28	29	30				

DECEMBER 2021

S	M	T	W	T	F	S
			1	2	3	4
5	6	7	8	9	10	11
12	13	14	15	16	17	18
19	20	21	22	23	24	25
26	27	28	29	30	31	

UNITED STATES FEDERAL HOLIDAYS & OBSERVANCES

January 1	New Year's Day	3rd Sunday in June	Father's Day
3rd Monday in January	Martin Luther King Day	July 4	Independence Day
January 23	National Pie Day	4th Sunday of July	Parent's Day
January 24	Global Belly Laugh Day	August 8	National CBD Day
February 1	National Freedom Day	August 19	National Aviation Day
February 2	Groundhog Day	1st Monday in September	Labor Day
February 9	National Pizza Day	1st Sunday after Labor Day	National Grandparent's Day
February 12	Lincoln's Birthday	September 11	Patriot Day
February 14	Valentine's Day	September 16	Stepfamily Day
3rd Monday in February	President's Day & Washington's Birthday	September 17	Constitution Day & Citizenship Day
March 17	St. Patrick's Day	3rd Friday of September	National POW/MIA Recognition Day
March 29	National Vietnam War Veterans Day	4th Friday of September	Native American Day
April 1	April Fool's Day	September 29	National Coffee Day
April 7	National Beer Day	2nd Monday in October	Columbus Day
April 13	Thomas Jefferson's Birthday	October 16	Boss's Day
April 15	Tax Day	3rd Saturday of October	Sweetest Day
April 22	Earth Day	October 31	Halloween
1st Thursday of May	National Day of Prayer	1st Tuesday of November	Election Day
2nd Sunday in May	Mother's Day	November 11	Veteran's Day
May 5	Cinco de Mayo	4th Thursday of the month	Thanksgiving
May 15	Peace Officers Memorial Day	December 7	Pearl Harbor Remembrance Day
3rd Saturday in May	Armed Forces Day	December 17	Wright Brother's Day
May 22	National Maritime Day	December 25	Christmas Day
1st Friday in June	National Donut Day	December 31	New Year's Eve

ATTENDANCE *Register*

	AUG	SEP	OCT	NOV	DEC	JAN	FEB	MAR	APR	MAY	JUNE	JULY
1												
2												
3												
4												
5												
6												
7												
8												
9												
10												
11												
12												
13												
14												
15												
16												
17												
18												
19												
20												
21												
22												
23												
24												
25												
26												
27												
28												
29												
30												
31												

SEMESTER ONE

AUGUST

Sunday	Monday	Tuesday	Wednesday
2	3	4	5
9	10	11	12
16	17	18	19
23　　　　30	24　　　　31	25	26

2020

Thursday	Friday	Saturday
		1
6	7	8
13	14	15
20	21	22
27	28	29

JULY 2020

S	M	T	W	T	F	S
			1	2	3	4
5	6	7	8	9	10	11
12	13	14	15	16	17	18
19	20	21	22	23	24	25
26	27	28	29	30	31	

LIST

- ○ _____
- ○ _____
- ○ _____
- ○ _____
- ○ _____
- ○ _____
- ○ _____
- ○ _____
- ○ _____
- ○ _____
- ○ _____

SEPTEMBER 2020

S	M	T	W	T	F	S
		1	2	3	4	5
6	7	8	9	10	11	12
13	14	15	16	17	18	19
20	21	22	23	24	25	26
27	28	29	30			

MONTHLY *Reading Register*

BOOK TITLE	DATE FINISHED

Reading Wish List

Weekly Plan

TO DO'S/ *Notes*

_____

_____

_____

_____

_____

_____

_____

_____

_____

_____

_____

_____

_____

_____

_____

_____

_____

_____

_____

_____

_____

_____

_____

Goals

Projects

19

Weekly Curriculum Plan

WEEK OF

SUBJECT	MON	TUES	WED	THUR	FRIDAY

SUBJECT	MON	TUES	WED	THUR	FRIDAY

SUBJECT	MON	TUES	WED	THUR	FRIDAY

SUBJECT	MON	TUES	WED	THUR	FRIDAY

SUBJECT	MON	TUES	WED	THUR	FRIDAY

SUBJECT	MON	TUES	WED	THUR	FRIDAY

Weekly ASSIGNMENTS

WEEK OF

✓
COMPLETED

- ○
- ○
- ○
- ○
- ○
- ○
- ○
- ○
- ○
- ○

Videos WATCHED

NAME OF MOVIE/VIDEO

NOTES

21

Weekly Plan

TO DO'S/ *Notes*

Goals

Projects

22

Weekly Curriculum Plan

WEEK OF

SUBJECT	MON	TUES	WED	THUR	FRIDAY

SUBJECT	MON	TUES	WED	THUR	FRIDAY

SUBJECT	MON	TUES	WED	THUR	FRIDAY

SUBJECT	MON	TUES	WED	THUR	FRIDAY

SUBJECT	MON	TUES	WED	THUR	FRIDAY

SUBJECT	MON	TUES	WED	THUR	FRIDAY

Weekly ASSIGNMENTS

WEEK OF _____

✓
COMPLETED

- ○
- ○
- ○
- ○
- ○
- ○
- ○
- ○
- ○
- ○

Videos WATCHED

NAME OF MOVIE/VIDEO

NOTES

Weekly Plan

TO DO'S/ *Notes*

_____

_____

_____

_____

_____

_____

_____

_____

_____

_____

_____

_____

_____

_____

_____

_____

_____

_____

_____

_____

_____

_____

_____

_____

Goals

Projects

25

Weekly Curriculum Plan

WEEK OF

SUBJECT	MON	TUES	WED	THUR	FRIDAY

SUBJECT	MON	TUES	WED	THUR	FRIDAY

SUBJECT	MON	TUES	WED	THUR	FRIDAY

SUBJECT	MON	TUES	WED	THUR	FRIDAY

SUBJECT	MON	TUES	WED	THUR	FRIDAY

SUBJECT	MON	TUES	WED	THUR	FRIDAY

Weekly ASSIGNMENTS

WEEK OF

✓
COMPLETED

- ○
- ○
- ○
- ○
- ○
- ○
- ○
- ○
- ○
- ○

Videos WATCHED

NAME OF MOVIE/VIDEO

NOTES

Weekly Plan

TO DO'S/ Notes

Goals

Projects

28

Weekly Curriculum Plan

WEEK OF

SUBJECT	MON	TUES	WED	THUR	FRIDAY

SUBJECT	MON	TUES	WED	THUR	FRIDAY

SUBJECT	MON	TUES	WED	THUR	FRIDAY

SUBJECT	MON	TUES	WED	THUR	FRIDAY

SUBJECT	MON	TUES	WED	THUR	FRIDAY

SUBJECT	MON	TUES	WED	THUR	FRIDAY

Weekly ASSIGNMENTS

- ○
- ○
- ○
- ○
- ○
- ○
- ○
- ○
- ○
- ○

Videos WATCHED

NAME OF MOVIE/VIDEO

NOTES

Monthly RECAP

Stop stressing about...

Conversations

Ideas

Shopping list

-
-
-
-
-
-
-
-
-
-

Things to do

Explore and learn about...

SEPTEMBER

Sunday	Monday	Tuesday	Wednesday
		1	2
6	7 Labor Day	8	9 Patriot Day
13 Grandparents' Day	14	15	16 Stepfamily Day
20	21	22 First Day of Fall	23
27	28	29	30

2020

AUGUST 2020

S	M	T	W	T	F	S
						1
2	3	4	5	6	7	8
9	10	11	12	13	14	15
16	17	18	19	20	21	22
23	24	25	26	27	28	29
30	31					

Thursday	Friday	Saturday
3	4	5
10	11 Patriot Day	12
17 Citizenship Day	18	19
24	25 Native American Day	26

LIST

○ _____

○ _____

○ _____

○ _____

○ _____

○ _____

○ _____

○ _____

○ _____

○ _____

○ _____

OCTOBER 2020

S	M	T	W	T	F	S
				1	2	3
4	5	6	7	8	9	10
11	12	13	14	15	16	17
18	19	20	21	22	23	24
25	26	27	28	29	30	31

MONTHLY *Reading Register*

BOOK TITLE	DATE FINISHED

Reading Wish List

Weekly Plan

TO DO'S/ *Notes*

Goals

Projects

35

Weekly Curriculum Plan

WEEK OF

SUBJECT	MON	TUES	WED	THUR	FRIDAY

SUBJECT	MON	TUES	WED	THUR	FRIDAY

SUBJECT	MON	TUES	WED	THUR	FRIDAY

SUBJECT	MON	TUES	WED	THUR	FRIDAY

SUBJECT	MON	TUES	WED	THUR	FRIDAY

SUBJECT	MON	TUES	WED	THUR	FRIDAY

Weekly ASSIGNMENTS

WEEK OF

✓
COMPLETED

○
○
○
○
○
○
○
○
○
○

Videos WATCHED

NAME OF MOVIE/VIDEO

NOTES

Weekly Plan

TO DO'S/ *Notes*

_____
_____
_____
_____
_____
_____
_____
_____
_____
_____
_____
_____
_____
_____
_____
_____
_____
_____
_____
_____
_____
_____
_____
_____
_____

Goals

Projects

38

Weekly Curriculum Plan

WEEK OF

SUBJECT	MON	TUES	WED	THUR	FRIDAY

SUBJECT	MON	TUES	WED	THUR	FRIDAY

SUBJECT	MON	TUES	WED	THUR	FRIDAY

SUBJECT	MON	TUES	WED	THUR	FRIDAY

SUBJECT	MON	TUES	WED	THUR	FRIDAY

SUBJECT	MON	TUES	WED	THUR	FRIDAY

Weekly ASSIGNMENTS

✓
COMPLETED

○ _____
○ _____
○ _____
○ _____
○ _____
○ _____
○ _____
○ _____
○ _____
○ _____

Videos WATCHED

NAME OF MOVIE/VIDEO

_____
_____
_____
_____
_____
_____

NOTES

Weekly Plan

TO DO'S/ Notes

_____
_____
_____
_____
_____
_____
_____
_____
_____
_____
_____
_____
_____
_____
_____
_____
_____
_____
_____
_____
_____
_____
_____
_____
_____
_____

Goals

Projects

Weekly Curriculum Plan

SUBJECT	MON	TUES	WED	THUR	FRIDAY

SUBJECT	MON	TUES	WED	THUR	FRIDAY

SUBJECT	MON	TUES	WED	THUR	FRIDAY

SUBJECT	MON	TUES	WED	THUR	FRIDAY

SUBJECT	MON	TUES	WED	THUR	FRIDAY

SUBJECT	MON	TUES	WED	THUR	FRIDAY

Weekly ASSIGNMENTS

WEEK OF _____

✓
COMPLETED

- ○
- ○
- ○
- ○
- ○
- ○
- ○
- ○
- ○
- ○

Videos WATCHED

NAME OF MOVIE/VIDEO

NOTES

Weekly Plan

TO DO'S/ *Notes*

_____

_____

_____

_____

_____

_____

_____

_____

_____

_____

_____

_____

_____

_____

_____

_____

_____

_____

_____

_____

_____

_____

_____

_____

_____

_____

Goals

Projects

44

Weekly Curriculum Plan

WEEK OF

SUBJECT	MON	TUES	WED	THUR	FRIDAY

SUBJECT	MON	TUES	WED	THUR	FRIDAY

SUBJECT	MON	TUES	WED	THUR	FRIDAY

SUBJECT	MON	TUES	WED	THUR	FRIDAY

SUBJECT	MON	TUES	WED	THUR	FRIDAY

SUBJECT	MON	TUES	WED	THUR	FRIDAY

Weekly ASSIGNMENTS

WEEK OF

✓
COMPLETED

- ○
- ○
- ○
- ○
- ○
- ○
- ○
- ○
- ○
- ○

Videos WATCHED

NAME OF MOVIE/VIDEO

NOTES

Monthly RECAP

Stop stressing about...

Ideas

Conversations

Shopping list

- ●
- ●
- ●
- ●
- ●
- ●
- ●
- ●
- ●

Things to do

Explore and learn about...

OCTOBER

Sunday	Monday	Tuesday	Wednesday
4	5	6	7
11	12 Columbus Day	13	14
18	19	20	21
25	26	27	28

2020

SEPTEMBER 2020

S	M	T	W	T	F	S
		1	2	3	4	5
6	7	8	9	10	11	12
13	14	15	16	17	18	19
20	21	22	23	24	25	26
27	28	29	30			

Thursday	Friday	Saturday
1	2	3
8	9	10
15	16 Boss's Day	17 Sweetest Day
22	23	24
29	30	31 Halloween

LIST

○ _____

○ _____

○ _____

○ _____

○ _____

○ _____

○ _____

○ _____

○ _____

○ _____

○ _____

NOVEMBER 2020

S	M	T	W	T	F	S
1	2	3	4	5	6	7
8	9	10	11	12	13	14
15	16	17	18	19	20	21
22	23	24	25	26	27	28
29	30					

MONTHLY *Reading Register*

BOOK TITLE	DATE FINISHED

Reading Wish List

Weekly Plan

TO DO'S/ *Notes*

_____

_____

_____

_____

_____

_____

_____

_____

_____

_____

_____

_____

_____

_____

_____

_____

_____

_____

_____

_____

_____

_____

_____

_____

_____

Goals

Projects

51

Weekly Curriculum Plan

WEEK OF

SUBJECT	MON	TUES	WED	THUR	FRIDAY

SUBJECT	MON	TUES	WED	THUR	FRIDAY

SUBJECT	MON	TUES	WED	THUR	FRIDAY

SUBJECT	MON	TUES	WED	THUR	FRIDAY

SUBJECT	MON	TUES	WED	THUR	FRIDAY

SUBJECT	MON	TUES	WED	THUR	FRIDAY

Weekly ASSIGNMENTS

WEEK OF

✓
COMPLETED

○
○
○
○
○
○
○
○
○
○

Videos WATCHED

NAME OF MOVIE/VIDEO

NOTES

Weekly Plan

TO DO'S/ *Notes*

_____

_____

_____

_____

_____

_____

_____

_____

_____

_____

_____

_____

_____

_____

_____

_____

_____

_____

_____

_____

_____

_____

_____

Goals

Projects

54

Weekly Curriculum Plan

WEEK OF

SUBJECT	MON	TUES	WED	THUR	FRIDAY

SUBJECT	MON	TUES	WED	THUR	FRIDAY

SUBJECT	MON	TUES	WED	THUR	FRIDAY

SUBJECT	MON	TUES	WED	THUR	FRIDAY

SUBJECT	MON	TUES	WED	THUR	FRIDAY

SUBJECT	MON	TUES	WED	THUR	FRIDAY

Weekly ASSIGNMENTS

WEEK OF

✓
COMPLETED

- ○
- ○
- ○
- ○
- ○
- ○
- ○
- ○
- ○
- ○

Videos WATCHED

NAME OF MOVIE/VIDEO

NOTES

Weekly Plan

TO DO'S/ *Notes*

_____
_____
_____
_____
_____
_____
_____
_____
_____
_____
_____
_____
_____
_____
_____
_____
_____
_____
_____
_____
_____
_____
_____

Goals

Projects

57

Weekly Curriculum Plan

WEEK OF

SUBJECT	MON	TUES	WED	THUR	FRIDAY

SUBJECT	MON	TUES	WED	THUR	FRIDAY

SUBJECT	MON	TUES	WED	THUR	FRIDAY

SUBJECT	MON	TUES	WED	THUR	FRIDAY

SUBJECT	MON	TUES	WED	THUR	FRIDAY

SUBJECT	MON	TUES	WED	THUR	FRIDAY

Weekly ASSIGNMENTS

WEEK OF

✓
COMPLETED

- ○
- ○
- ○
- ○
- ○
- ○
- ○
- ○
- ○
- ○

Videos WATCHED

NAME OF MOVIE/VIDEO

NOTES

Weekly Plan

TO DO'S/ *Notes*

_____

_____

_____

_____

_____

_____

_____

_____

_____

_____

_____

_____

_____

_____

_____

_____

_____

_____

_____

_____

_____

_____

Goals

Projects

60

Weekly Curriculum Plan

WEEK OF

SUBJECT	MON	TUES	WED	THUR	FRIDAY

SUBJECT	MON	TUES	WED	THUR	FRIDAY

SUBJECT	MON	TUES	WED	THUR	FRIDAY

SUBJECT	MON	TUES	WED	THUR	FRIDAY

SUBJECT	MON	TUES	WED	THUR	FRIDAY

SUBJECT	MON	TUES	WED	THUR	FRIDAY

Weekly ASSIGNMENTS

WEEK OF

✓
COMPLETED

- ○
- ○
- ○
- ○
- ○
- ○
- ○
- ○
- ○
- ○

Videos WATCHED

NAME OF MOVIE/VIDEO

NOTES

Monthly RECAP

Stop stressing about...

Ideas

Conversations

Shopping list

Things to do

-
-
-
-
-
-
-
-
-

Explore and learn about...

NOVEMBER

Sunday	Monday	Tuesday	Wednesday
1 Daylight Saving Ends	2	3	4
8	9	10	11 Veteran's Day
15	16	17	18
22	23	24	25
29	30 Cyber Monday		

2020

Thursday	Friday	Saturday
5	6	7
12	13	14
19	20	21
26 Thanksgiving	27 Black Friday	28

S	M	T	W	T	F	S
				1	2	3
4	5	6	7	8	9	10
11	12	13	14	15	16	17
18	19	20	21	22	23	24
25	26	27	28	29	30	31

LIST

○ _____

○ _____

○ _____

○ _____

○ _____

○ _____

○ _____

○ _____

○ _____

○ _____

○ _____

DECEMBER 2020

S	M	T	W	T	F	S
		1	2	3	4	5
6	7	8	9	10	11	12
13	14	15	16	17	18	19
20	21	22	23	24	25	26
27	28	29	30	31		

MONTHLY *Reading Register*

BOOK TITLE	DATE FINISHED

Reading Wish List

Weekly Plan

TO DO'S/ *Notes*

_____

_____

_____

_____

_____

_____

_____

_____

_____

_____

_____

_____

_____

_____

_____

_____

_____

_____

_____

_____

_____

Goals

Projects

67

Weekly Curriculum Plan

WEEK OF

SUBJECT	MON	TUES	WED	THUR	FRIDAY

SUBJECT	MON	TUES	WED	THUR	FRIDAY

SUBJECT	MON	TUES	WED	THUR	FRIDAY

SUBJECT	MON	TUES	WED	THUR	FRIDAY

SUBJECT	MON	TUES	WED	THUR	FRIDAY

SUBJECT	MON	TUES	WED	THUR	FRIDAY

Weekly ASSIGNMENTS

WEEK OF

✓
COMPLETED

- ○
- ○
- ○
- ○
- ○
- ○
- ○
- ○
- ○
- ○

Videos WATCHED

NAME OF MOVIE/VIDEO

NOTES

Weekly Plan

TO DO'S/ *Notes*

_____
_____
_____
_____
_____
_____
_____
_____
_____
_____
_____
_____
_____
_____
_____
_____
_____
_____
_____
_____
_____
_____
_____
_____
_____
_____

Goals

Projects

70

Weekly Curriculum Plan

WEEK OF

SUBJECT	MON	TUES	WED	THUR	FRIDAY

SUBJECT	MON	TUES	WED	THUR	FRIDAY

SUBJECT	MON	TUES	WED	THUR	FRIDAY

SUBJECT	MON	TUES	WED	THUR	FRIDAY

SUBJECT	MON	TUES	WED	THUR	FRIDAY

SUBJECT	MON	TUES	WED	THUR	FRIDAY

Weekly ASSIGNMENTS

WEEK OF

✓
COMPLETED

- ○
- ○
- ○
- ○
- ○
- ○
- ○
- ○
- ○
- ○

Videos WATCHED

NAME OF MOVIE/VIDEO

NOTES

Weekly Plan

TO DO'S/ *Notes*

_____
_____
_____
_____
_____
_____
_____
_____
_____
_____
_____
_____
_____
_____
_____
_____
_____
_____
_____
_____
_____
_____
_____

Goals

Projects

73

Weekly Curriculum Plan

WEEK OF

SUBJECT	MON	TUES	WED	THUR	FRIDAY

SUBJECT	MON	TUES	WED	THUR	FRIDAY

SUBJECT	MON	TUES	WED	THUR	FRIDAY

SUBJECT	MON	TUES	WED	THUR	FRIDAY

SUBJECT	MON	TUES	WED	THUR	FRIDAY

SUBJECT	MON	TUES	WED	THUR	FRIDAY

Weekly ASSIGNMENTS

WEEK OF

✓
COMPLETED

○
○
○
○
○
○
○
○
○
○

Videos WATCHED

NAME OF MOVIE/VIDEO

NOTES

Weekly Plan

TO DO'S/ *Notes*

_____

_____

_____

_____

_____

_____

_____

_____

_____

_____

_____

_____

_____

_____

_____

_____

_____

_____

_____

_____

_____

_____

_____

Goals

Projects

76

Weekly Curriculum Plan

SUBJECT	MON	TUES	WED	THUR	FRIDAY

SUBJECT	MON	TUES	WED	THUR	FRIDAY

SUBJECT	MON	TUES	WED	THUR	FRIDAY

SUBJECT	MON	TUES	WED	THUR	FRIDAY

SUBJECT	MON	TUES	WED	THUR	FRIDAY

SUBJECT	MON	TUES	WED	THUR	FRIDAY

Weekly ASSIGNMENTS

WEEK OF

✓
COMPLETED

○
○
○
○
○
○
○
○
○
○

Videos WATCHED

NAME OF MOVIE/VIDEO

NOTES

Monthly RECAP

Stop stressing about...

Ideas

Conversations

Things to do

Shopping list

-
-
-
-
-
-
-
-
-

Explore and learn about...

DECEMBER

Sunday	Monday	Tuesday	Wednesday
		1	2
6	7 Pearl Harbor Day	8	9
13	14	15	16
20	21 First Day of Winter	22	23
27	28	29	30

2020

S	M	T	W	T	F	S
1	2	3	4	5	6	7
8	9	10	11	12	13	14
15	16	17	18	19	20	21
22	23	24	25	26	27	28
29	30					

Thursday	Friday	Saturday
3	4	5
10	11	12
17	18	19
24	25 Christmas Day	26
31 New Year's Eve		

LIST

○ _____

○ _____

○ _____

○ _____

○ _____

○ _____

○ _____

○ _____

○ _____

○ _____

○ _____

JANUARY 2021

S	M	T	W	T	F	S
					1	2
3	4	5	6	7	8	9
10	11	12	13	14	15	16
17	18	19	20	21	22	23
24	25	26	27	28	29	30
31						

MONTHLY *Reading Register*

BOOK TITLE	DATE FINISHED

Reading Wish List

Weekly Plan

TO DO'S/ *Notes*

_____
_____
_____
_____
_____
_____
_____
_____
_____
_____
_____
_____
_____
_____
_____
_____
_____
_____
_____
_____
_____
_____

Goals

Projects

Weekly Curriculum Plan

WEEK OF

SUBJECT	MON	TUES	WED	THUR	FRIDAY

SUBJECT	MON	TUES	WED	THUR	FRIDAY

SUBJECT	MON	TUES	WED	THUR	FRIDAY

SUBJECT	MON	TUES	WED	THUR	FRIDAY

SUBJECT	MON	TUES	WED	THUR	FRIDAY

SUBJECT	MON	TUES	WED	THUR	FRIDAY

Weekly ASSIGNMENTS

WEEK OF

✓
COMPLETED

- ○
- ○
- ○
- ○
- ○
- ○
- ○
- ○
- ○
- ○

Videos WATCHED

NAME OF MOVIE/VIDEO

NOTES

Weekly Plan

TO DO'S/ *Notes*

_____
_____
_____
_____
_____
_____
_____
_____
_____
_____
_____
_____
_____
_____
_____
_____
_____
_____
_____
_____
_____
_____
_____
_____
_____

Goals

Projects

86

Weekly Curriculum Plan

WEEK OF

SUBJECT	MON	TUES	WED	THUR	FRIDAY

SUBJECT	MON	TUES	WED	THUR	FRIDAY

SUBJECT	MON	TUES	WED	THUR	FRIDAY

SUBJECT	MON	TUES	WED	THUR	FRIDAY

SUBJECT	MON	TUES	WED	THUR	FRIDAY

SUBJECT	MON	TUES	WED	THUR	FRIDAY

Weekly ASSIGNMENTS

WEEK OF

✓
COMPLETED

- ○ _____
- ○ _____
- ○ _____
- ○ _____
- ○ _____
- ○ _____
- ○ _____
- ○ _____
- ○ _____
- ○ _____

Videos WATCHED

NAME OF MOVIE/VIDEO

_____

_____

_____

_____

_____

_____

NOTES

Weekly Plan

TO DO'S/ *Notes*

_____
_____
_____
_____
_____
_____
_____
_____
_____
_____
_____
_____
_____
_____
_____
_____
_____
_____
_____
_____
_____
_____

Goals

Projects

Weekly Curriculum Plan

WEEK OF

SUBJECT	MON	TUES	WED	THUR	FRIDAY

SUBJECT	MON	TUES	WED	THUR	FRIDAY

SUBJECT	MON	TUES	WED	THUR	FRIDAY

SUBJECT	MON	TUES	WED	THUR	FRIDAY

SUBJECT	MON	TUES	WED	THUR	FRIDAY

SUBJECT	MON	TUES	WED	THUR	FRIDAY

Weekly ASSIGNMENTS

WEEK OF

✓
COMPLETED

○
○
○
○
○
○
○
○
○
○

Videos WATCHED

NAME OF MOVIE/VIDEO

NOTES

Weekly Plan

TO DO'S/ *Notes*

_____
_____
_____
_____
_____
_____
_____
_____
_____
_____
_____
_____
_____
_____
_____
_____
_____
_____
_____
_____
_____
_____
_____

Goals

Projects

92

Weekly Curriculum Plan

WEEK OF

SUBJECT	MON	TUES	WED	THUR	FRIDAY

SUBJECT	MON	TUES	WED	THUR	FRIDAY

SUBJECT	MON	TUES	WED	THUR	FRIDAY

SUBJECT	MON	TUES	WED	THUR	FRIDAY

SUBJECT	MON	TUES	WED	THUR	FRIDAY

SUBJECT	MON	TUES	WED	THUR	FRIDAY

Weekly ASSIGNMENTS

WEEK OF _____

✓
COMPLETED

- ○
- ○
- ○
- ○
- ○
- ○
- ○
- ○
- ○
- ○

Videos WATCHED

NAME OF MOVIE/VIDEO

NOTES

Monthly RECAP

Stop stressing about...

Ideas

Conversations

Shopping list

-
-
-
-
-
-
-
-
-
-

Things to do

Explore and learn about...

GRADE REGISTER | *Semester 1*

SUBJECT: _____

Date	Assignment or Test	Points Possible	Points Achieved	Grade
		Semester 1 Grade		

SUBJECT: _____

Date	Assignment or Test	Points Possible	Points Achieved	Grade
		Semester 1 Grade		

GRADE REGISTER | *Semester 1*

SUBJECT: _____

Date	Assignment or Test	Points Possible	Points Achieved	Grade
		Semester 1 Grade		

SUBJECT: _____

Date	Assignment or Test	Points Possible	Points Achieved	Grade
		Semester 1 Grade		

GRADE REGISTER | Semester 1

SUBJECT: _____

Date	Assignment or Test	Points Possible	Points Achieved	Grade
	Semester 1 Grade			

SUBJECT: _____

Date	Assignment or Test	Points Possible	Points Achieved	Grade
	Semester 1 Grade			

GRADE REGISTER | Semester 1

SUBJECT: _____

Date	Assignment or Test	Points Possible	Points Achieved	Grade
		Semester 1 Grade		

SUBJECT: _____

Date	Assignment or Test	Points Possible	Points Achieved	Grade
		Semester 1 Grade		

1ST SEMESTER *Student Reflections*

SUCCESSES:

HABITS:

CHARACTER:

WHAT CAN WE DO BETTER?

OTHER NOTES:

SEMESTER TWO

JANUARY

Sunday	Monday	Tuesday	Wednesday
3	4	5	6
10	11	12	13
17	18 Martin Luther King Jr. Day	19	20
24 31	25	26	27

2021

Thursday	Friday	Saturday
	1 New Year's Day	2
7	8	9
14	15	16
21	22	23 National Pie Day
28	29	30

DECEMBER 2020

S	M	T	W	T	F	S
		1	2	3	4	5
6	7	8	9	10	11	12
13	14	15	16	17	18	19
20	21	22	23	24	25	26
27	28	29	30	31		

LIST

○ _____

○ _____

○ _____

○ _____

○ _____

○ _____

○ _____

○ _____

○ _____

○ _____

○ _____

FEBRUARY 2021

S	M	T	W	T	F	S
	1	2	3	4	5	6
7	8	9	10	11	12	13
14	15	16	17	18	19	20
21	22	23	24	25	26	27
28						

MONTHLY *Reading Register*

BOOK TITLE	DATE FINISHED

Reading Wish List

Weekly Plan

TO DO'S/*Notes*

_____
_____
_____
_____
_____
_____
_____
_____
_____
_____
_____
_____
_____
_____
_____
_____
_____
_____
_____
_____
_____
_____
_____
_____
_____
_____

Goals

Projects

Weekly Curriculum Plan

SUBJECT	MON	TUES	WED	THUR	FRIDAY

SUBJECT	MON	TUES	WED	THUR	FRIDAY

SUBJECT	MON	TUES	WED	THUR	FRIDAY

SUBJECT	MON	TUES	WED	THUR	FRIDAY

SUBJECT	MON	TUES	WED	THUR	FRIDAY

SUBJECT	MON	TUES	WED	THUR	FRIDAY

Weekly ASSIGNMENTS

✓
COMPLETED

- ○
- ○
- ○
- ○
- ○
- ○
- ○
- ○
- ○
- ○

Videos WATCHED

NAME OF MOVIE/VIDEO

NOTES

107

Weekly Plan

TO DO'S/ *Notes*

Goals

Projects

Weekly Curriculum Plan

WEEK OF

SUBJECT	MON	TUES	WED	THUR	FRIDAY

SUBJECT	MON	TUES	WED	THUR	FRIDAY

SUBJECT	MON	TUES	WED	THUR	FRIDAY

SUBJECT	MON	TUES	WED	THUR	FRIDAY

SUBJECT	MON	TUES	WED	THUR	FRIDAY

SUBJECT	MON	TUES	WED	THUR	FRIDAY

Weekly ASSIGNMENTS

WEEK OF

✓
COMPLETED

- ○
- ○
- ○
- ○
- ○
- ○
- ○
- ○
- ○
- ○

Videos WATCHED

NAME OF MOVIE/VIDEO

NOTES

Weekly Plan

TO DO'S/ *Notes*

_____
_____
_____
_____
_____
_____
_____
_____
_____
_____
_____
_____
_____
_____
_____
_____
_____
_____
_____
_____
_____
_____
_____
_____

Goals

Projects

111

Weekly Curriculum Plan

WEEK OF

SUBJECT	MON	TUES	WED	THUR	FRIDAY

SUBJECT	MON	TUES	WED	THUR	FRIDAY

SUBJECT	MON	TUES	WED	THUR	FRIDAY

SUBJECT	MON	TUES	WED	THUR	FRIDAY

SUBJECT	MON	TUES	WED	THUR	FRIDAY

SUBJECT	MON	TUES	WED	THUR	FRIDAY

Weekly ASSIGNMENTS

WEEK OF

✓
COMPLETED

- ○
- ○
- ○
- ○
- ○
- ○
- ○
- ○
- ○
- ○

Videos WATCHED

NAME OF MOVIE/VIDEO

NOTES

Weekly Plan

TO DO'S/ *Notes*

_____
_____
_____
_____
_____
_____
_____
_____
_____
_____
_____
_____
_____
_____
_____
_____
_____
_____
_____
_____
_____
_____

Goals

Projects

114

Weekly Curriculum Plan

WEEK OF

SUBJECT	MON	TUES	WED	THUR	FRIDAY

SUBJECT	MON	TUES	WED	THUR	FRIDAY

SUBJECT	MON	TUES	WED	THUR	FRIDAY

SUBJECT	MON	TUES	WED	THUR	FRIDAY

SUBJECT	MON	TUES	WED	THUR	FRIDAY

SUBJECT	MON	TUES	WED	THUR	FRIDAY

Weekly ASSIGNMENTS

✓
COMPLETED

○ _____
○ _____
○ _____
○ _____
○ _____
○ _____
○ _____
○ _____
○ _____
○ _____

Videos WATCHED

NAME OF MOVIE/VIDEO

_____
_____
_____
_____
_____
_____

NOTES

Monthly RECAP

Stop stressing about...

Ideas

Conversations

Shopping list

-
-
-
-
-
-
-
-
-
-

Things to do

Explore and learn about...

FEBRUARY

Sunday	Monday	Tuesday	Wednesday
	1 National Freedom Day	2 Ground Hog Day	3
7	8	9 National Pizza Day	10
14	15	16	17
21 President's Day Washington's Birthday	22	23	24
28			

2021

Thursday	Friday	Saturday
4	5	6
11	12 Lincoln's Birthday	13
18	19	20
25	26	27

JANUARY 2021

S	M	T	W	T	F	S
					1	2
3	4	5	6	7	8	9
10	11	12	13	14	15	16
17	18	19	20	21	22	23
24	25	26	27	28	29	30
31						

LIST

○ _____

○ _____

○ _____

○ _____

○ _____

○ _____

○ _____

○ _____

○ _____

○ _____

○ _____

MARCH 2021

S	M	T	W	T	F	S
	1	2	3	4	5	6
7	8	9	10	11	12	13
14	15	16	17	18	19	20
21	22	23	24	25	26	27
28	29	30	31			

MONTHLY *Reading Register*

BOOK TITLE	DATE FINISHED

Reading Wish List

Weekly Plan

TO DO'S/ *Notes*

Goals

Projects

Weekly Curriculum Plan

WEEK OF

SUBJECT	MON	TUES	WED	THUR	FRIDAY

SUBJECT	MON	TUES	WED	THUR	FRIDAY

SUBJECT	MON	TUES	WED	THUR	FRIDAY

SUBJECT	MON	TUES	WED	THUR	FRIDAY

SUBJECT	MON	TUES	WED	THUR	FRIDAY

SUBJECT	MON	TUES	WED	THUR	FRIDAY

Weekly ASSIGNMENTS

WEEK OF

✓
COMPLETED

- ○
- ○
- ○
- ○
- ○
- ○
- ○
- ○
- ○
- ○

Videos WATCHED

NAME OF MOVIE/VIDEO

NOTES

Weekly Plan

TO DO'S/ *Notes*

_____
_____
_____
_____
_____
_____
_____
_____
_____
_____
_____
_____
_____
_____
_____
_____
_____
_____
_____
_____
_____
_____
_____
_____
_____

Goals

Projects

124

Weekly Curriculum Plan

WEEK OF

SUBJECT	MON	TUES	WED	THUR	FRIDAY

SUBJECT	MON	TUES	WED	THUR	FRIDAY

SUBJECT	MON	TUES	WED	THUR	FRIDAY

SUBJECT	MON	TUES	WED	THUR	FRIDAY

SUBJECT	MON	TUES	WED	THUR	FRIDAY

SUBJECT	MON	TUES	WED	THUR	FRIDAY

Weekly ASSIGNMENTS

WEEK OF

✓
COMPLETED

- ○
- ○
- ○
- ○
- ○
- ○
- ○
- ○
- ○
- ○

Videos WATCHED

NAME OF MOVIE/VIDEO

NOTES

Weekly Plan

TO DO'S/ *Notes*

_____
_____
_____
_____
_____
_____
_____
_____
_____
_____
_____
_____
_____
_____
_____
_____
_____
_____
_____
_____
_____
_____
_____
_____
_____

Goals

Projects

Weekly Curriculum Plan

WEEK OF

SUBJECT	MON	TUES	WED	THUR	FRIDAY

SUBJECT	MON	TUES	WED	THUR	FRIDAY

SUBJECT	MON	TUES	WED	THUR	FRIDAY

SUBJECT	MON	TUES	WED	THUR	FRIDAY

SUBJECT	MON	TUES	WED	THUR	FRIDAY

SUBJECT	MON	TUES	WED	THUR	FRIDAY

Weekly ASSIGNMENTS

- ○
- ○
- ○
- ○
- ○
- ○
- ○
- ○
- ○
- ○

Videos WATCHED

NAME OF MOVIE/VIDEO

NOTES

Weekly Plan

TO DO'S/ *Notes*

_____
_____
_____
_____
_____
_____
_____
_____
_____
_____
_____
_____
_____
_____
_____
_____
_____
_____
_____
_____
_____
_____
_____
_____
_____
_____

Goals

Projects

130

Weekly Curriculum Plan

WEEK OF

SUBJECT	MON	TUES	WED	THUR	FRIDAY

SUBJECT	MON	TUES	WED	THUR	FRIDAY

SUBJECT	MON	TUES	WED	THUR	FRIDAY

SUBJECT	MON	TUES	WED	THUR	FRIDAY

SUBJECT	MON	TUES	WED	THUR	FRIDAY

SUBJECT	MON	TUES	WED	THUR	FRIDAY

Weekly ASSIGNMENTS

WEEK OF

✓
COMPLETED

- ○
- ○
- ○
- ○
- ○
- ○
- ○
- ○
- ○
- ○

Videos WATCHED

NAME OF MOVIE/VIDEO

NOTES

Monthly RECAP

Stop stressing about...

Ideas

Conversations

Things to do

Shopping list

-
-
-
-
-
-
-
-
-

Explore and learn about...

MARCH

Sunday	Monday	Tuesday	Wednesday
	1	2	3
7	8	9	10
14	15	16	17 St. Patrick's Day
21	22	23	24
28	29 National Vietnam War Veterans Day	30	31

2021

FEBRUARY 2021

S	M	T	W	T	F	S
	1	2	3	4	5	6
7	8	9	10	11	12	13
14	15	16	17	18	19	20
21	22	23	24	25	26	27
28						

Thursday	Friday	Saturday
4	5	6
11	12	13
18	19	20
25	26	27

LIST

- ○ _____
- ○ _____
- ○ _____
- ○ _____
- ○ _____
- ○ _____
- ○ _____
- ○ _____
- ○ _____
- ○ _____
- ○ _____

APRIL 2021

S	M	T	W	T	F	S
				1	2	3
4	5	6	7	8	9	10
11	12	13	14	15	16	17
18	19	20	21	22	23	24
25	26	27	28	29	30	

MONTHLY *Reading Register*

BOOK TITLE	DATE FINISHED

Reading Wish List

_____

_____

_____

_____

Weekly Plan

TO DO'S/ *Notes*

Goals

Projects

137

Weekly Curriculum Plan

WEEK OF

SUBJECT	MON	TUES	WED	THUR	FRIDAY

SUBJECT	MON	TUES	WED	THUR	FRIDAY

SUBJECT	MON	TUES	WED	THUR	FRIDAY

SUBJECT	MON	TUES	WED	THUR	FRIDAY

SUBJECT	MON	TUES	WED	THUR	FRIDAY

SUBJECT	MON	TUES	WED	THUR	FRIDAY

Weekly ASSIGNMENTS

WEEK OF _____

✓ COMPLETED

- ○
- ○
- ○
- ○
- ○
- ○
- ○
- ○
- ○
- ○

Videos WATCHED

NAME OF MOVIE/VIDEO

NOTES

Weekly Plan

TO DO'S/ *Notes*

_____

_____

_____

_____

_____

_____

_____

_____

_____

_____

_____

_____

_____

_____

_____

_____

_____

_____

_____

_____

_____

_____

_____

Goals

Projects

140

Weekly Curriculum Plan

WEEK OF

SUBJECT	MON	TUES	WED	THUR	FRIDAY

SUBJECT	MON	TUES	WED	THUR	FRIDAY

SUBJECT	MON	TUES	WED	THUR	FRIDAY

SUBJECT	MON	TUES	WED	THUR	FRIDAY

SUBJECT	MON	TUES	WED	THUR	FRIDAY

SUBJECT	MON	TUES	WED	THUR	FRIDAY

Weekly ASSIGNMENTS

WEEK OF

✓ COMPLETED

- ○
- ○
- ○
- ○
- ○
- ○
- ○
- ○
- ○
- ○

Videos WATCHED

NAME OF MOVIE/VIDEO

NOTES

Weekly Plan

TO DO'S/ *Notes*

Goals

Projects

143

Weekly Curriculum Plan

WEEK OF

SUBJECT	MON	TUES	WED	THUR	FRIDAY

SUBJECT	MON	TUES	WED	THUR	FRIDAY

SUBJECT	MON	TUES	WED	THUR	FRIDAY

SUBJECT	MON	TUES	WED	THUR	FRIDAY

SUBJECT	MON	TUES	WED	THUR	FRIDAY

SUBJECT	MON	TUES	WED	THUR	FRIDAY

Weekly ASSIGNMENTS

WEEK OF

✓
COMPLETED

- ○
- ○
- ○
- ○
- ○
- ○
- ○
- ○
- ○
- ○

Videos WATCHED

NAME OF MOVIE/VIDEO

NOTES

Weekly Plan

TO DO'S/ *Notes*

_____

_____

_____

_____

_____

_____

_____

_____

_____

_____

_____

_____

_____

_____

_____

_____

_____

_____

_____

_____

_____

_____

_____

Goals

Projects

Weekly Curriculum Plan

WEEK OF

SUBJECT	MON	TUES	WED	THUR	FRIDAY

SUBJECT	MON	TUES	WED	THUR	FRIDAY

SUBJECT	MON	TUES	WED	THUR	FRIDAY

SUBJECT	MON	TUES	WED	THUR	FRIDAY

SUBJECT	MON	TUES	WED	THUR	FRIDAY

SUBJECT	MON	TUES	WED	THUR	FRIDAY

Weekly ASSIGNMENTS

WEEK OF

✓
COMPLETED

- ○
- ○
- ○
- ○
- ○
- ○
- ○
- ○
- ○
- ○

Videos WATCHED

NAME OF MOVIE/VIDEO

NOTES

Monthly RECAP

Stop stressing about...

Ideas

Conversations

Shopping list

- •
- •
- •
- •
- •
- •
- •
- •
- •

Things to do

Explore and learn about...

APRIL

Sunday	Monday	Tuesday	Wednesday
4 Easter	5	6	7
11	12	13 Thomas Jefferson's Birthday	14
18	19	20	21
25	26	27	28

2021

MARCH 2021

S	M	T	W	T	F	S
	1	2	3	4	5	6
7	8	9	10	11	12	13
14	15	16	17	18	19	20
21	22	23	24	25	26	27
28	29	30	31			

Thursday	Friday	Saturday
1 April Fool's Day	2 Good Friday	3
8	9	10
15 Tax Day	16	17
22 Earth Day	23	24
29	30	

LIST

○ _____

○ _____

○ _____

○ _____

○ _____

○ _____

○ _____

○ _____

○ _____

○ _____

○ _____

MAY 2021

S	M	T	W	T	F	S
						1
2	3	4	5	6	7	8
9	10	11	12	13	14	15
16	17	18	19	20	21	22
23	24	25	26	27	28	29
30	31					

MONTHLY *Reading Register*

BOOK TITLE	DATE FINISHED

Reading Wish List

Weekly Plan

TO DO'S/ *Notes*

Goals

Projects

153

Weekly Curriculum Plan

WEEK OF

SUBJECT	MON	TUES	WED	THUR	FRIDAY

SUBJECT	MON	TUES	WED	THUR	FRIDAY

SUBJECT	MON	TUES	WED	THUR	FRIDAY

SUBJECT	MON	TUES	WED	THUR	FRIDAY

SUBJECT	MON	TUES	WED	THUR	FRIDAY

SUBJECT	MON	TUES	WED	THUR	FRIDAY

Weekly ASSIGNMENTS

WEEK OF

✓
COMPLETED

- ○
- ○
- ○
- ○
- ○
- ○
- ○
- ○
- ○
- ○

Videos WATCHED

NAME OF MOVIE/VIDEO

NOTES

Weekly Plan

TO DO'S/ *Notes*

_____
_____
_____
_____
_____
_____
_____
_____
_____
_____
_____
_____
_____
_____
_____
_____
_____
_____
_____
_____
_____
_____
_____
_____

Goals

Projects

156

Weekly Curriculum Plan

WEEK OF

SUBJECT	MON	TUES	WED	THUR	FRIDAY

SUBJECT	MON	TUES	WED	THUR	FRIDAY

SUBJECT	MON	TUES	WED	THUR	FRIDAY

SUBJECT	MON	TUES	WED	THUR	FRIDAY

SUBJECT	MON	TUES	WED	THUR	FRIDAY

SUBJECT	MON	TUES	WED	THUR	FRIDAY

Weekly ASSIGNMENTS

WEEK OF

✓
COMPLETED

- ○
- ○
- ○
- ○
- ○
- ○
- ○
- ○
- ○
- ○

Videos WATCHED

NAME OF MOVIE/VIDEO

NOTES

Weekly Plan

TO DO'S/ *Notes*

_____

_____

_____

_____

_____

_____

_____

_____

_____

_____

_____

_____

_____

_____

_____

_____

_____

_____

_____

_____

_____

_____

_____

Goals

Projects

Weekly Curriculum Plan

WEEK OF

SUBJECT	MON	TUES	WED	THUR	FRIDAY

SUBJECT	MON	TUES	WED	THUR	FRIDAY

SUBJECT	MON	TUES	WED	THUR	FRIDAY

SUBJECT	MON	TUES	WED	THUR	FRIDAY

SUBJECT	MON	TUES	WED	THUR	FRIDAY

SUBJECT	MON	TUES	WED	THUR	FRIDAY

Weekly ASSIGNMENTS

✓
COMPLETED

- ○
- ○
- ○
- ○
- ○
- ○
- ○
- ○
- ○
- ○

Videos WATCHED

NAME OF MOVIE/VIDEO

NOTES

Weekly Plan

TO DO'S/ *Notes*

_____

_____

_____

_____

_____

_____

_____

_____

_____

_____

_____

_____

_____

_____

_____

_____

_____

_____

_____

_____

_____

_____

_____

_____

Goals

Projects

Weekly Curriculum Plan

WEEK OF

SUBJECT	MON	TUES	WED	THUR	FRIDAY

SUBJECT	MON	TUES	WED	THUR	FRIDAY

SUBJECT	MON	TUES	WED	THUR	FRIDAY

SUBJECT	MON	TUES	WED	THUR	FRIDAY

SUBJECT	MON	TUES	WED	THUR	FRIDAY

SUBJECT	MON	TUES	WED	THUR	FRIDAY

Weekly ASSIGNMENTS

WEEK OF

✓
COMPLETED

- ○
- ○
- ○
- ○
- ○
- ○
- ○
- ○
- ○
- ○

Videos WATCHED

NAME OF MOVIE/VIDEO

NOTES

Monthly RECAP

Stop stressing about...

Ideas

Conversations

Shopping list

-
-
-
-
-
-
-
-
-

Things to do

Explore and learn about...

MAY

Sunday	Monday	Tuesday	Wednesday
2	3	4	5 Cinco de Mayo
9 Mother's Day	10	11	12
16	17	18	19
23 30	24 31	25	26

2021

APRIL 2021

S	M	T	W	T	F	S
				1	2	3
4	5	6	7	8	9	10
11	12	13	14	15	16	17
18	19	20	21	22	23	24
25	26	27	28	29	30	

Thursday	Friday	Saturday
		1
6 National Day of Prayer	7	8
13	14	15 Armed Forces Day Peace Officer's Memorial Day
20	21	22 National Maritime Day
27	28	29

LIST

○ _____
○ _____
○ _____
○ _____
○ _____
○ _____
○ _____
○ _____
○ _____
○ _____
○ _____

JUNE 2021

S	M	T	W	T	F	S
		1	2	3	4	5
6	7	8	9	10	11	12
13	14	15	16	17	18	19
20	21	22	23	24	25	26
27	28	29	30			

MONTHLY *Reading Register*

BOOK TITLE	DATE FINISHED

Reading Wish List

Weekly Plan

TO DO'S/ *Notes*

_____
_____
_____
_____
_____
_____
_____
_____
_____
_____
_____
_____
_____
_____
_____
_____
_____
_____
_____
_____
_____
_____
_____
_____
_____

Goals

Projects

169

Weekly Curriculum Plan

WEEK OF _____

SUBJECT	MON	TUES	WED	THUR	FRIDAY

SUBJECT	MON	TUES	WED	THUR	FRIDAY

SUBJECT	MON	TUES	WED	THUR	FRIDAY

SUBJECT	MON	TUES	WED	THUR	FRIDAY

SUBJECT	MON	TUES	WED	THUR	FRIDAY

SUBJECT	MON	TUES	WED	THUR	FRIDAY

Weekly ASSIGNMENTS

WEEK OF

✓
COMPLETED

- ○
- ○
- ○
- ○
- ○
- ○
- ○
- ○
- ○
- ○

Videos WATCHED

NAME OF MOVIE/VIDEO

NOTES

Weekly Plan

TO DO'S/ *Notes*

_____
_____
_____
_____
_____
_____
_____
_____
_____
_____
_____
_____
_____
_____
_____
_____
_____
_____
_____
_____
_____
_____
_____
_____
_____
_____

Goals

Projects

172

Weekly Curriculum Plan

WEEK OF

SUBJECT	MON	TUES	WED	THUR	FRIDAY

SUBJECT	MON	TUES	WED	THUR	FRIDAY

SUBJECT	MON	TUES	WED	THUR	FRIDAY

SUBJECT	MON	TUES	WED	THUR	FRIDAY

SUBJECT	MON	TUES	WED	THUR	FRIDAY

SUBJECT	MON	TUES	WED	THUR	FRIDAY

Weekly ASSIGNMENTS

WEEK OF

✓
COMPLETED

- ○
- ○
- ○
- ○
- ○
- ○
- ○
- ○
- ○
- ○

Videos WATCHED

NAME OF MOVIE/VIDEO

NOTES

Weekly Plan

TO DO'S/ *Notes*

_____
_____
_____
_____
_____
_____
_____
_____
_____
_____
_____
_____
_____
_____
_____
_____
_____
_____
_____
_____
_____
_____
_____
_____

Goals

Projects

Weekly Curriculum Plan

WEEK OF

SUBJECT	MON	TUES	WED	THUR	FRIDAY

SUBJECT	MON	TUES	WED	THUR	FRIDAY

SUBJECT	MON	TUES	WED	THUR	FRIDAY

SUBJECT	MON	TUES	WED	THUR	FRIDAY

SUBJECT	MON	TUES	WED	THUR	FRIDAY

SUBJECT	MON	TUES	WED	THUR	FRIDAY

Weekly ASSIGNMENTS

WEEK OF _____

✓
COMPLETED

- ○
- ○
- ○
- ○
- ○
- ○
- ○
- ○
- ○
- ○

Videos WATCHED

NAME OF MOVIE/VIDEO

NOTES

Weekly Plan

TO DO'S/ *Notes*

_____

_____

_____

_____

_____

_____

_____

_____

_____

_____

_____

_____

_____

_____

_____

_____

_____

_____

_____

_____

Goals

Projects

Weekly Curriculum Plan

WEEK OF

SUBJECT	MON	TUES	WED	THUR	FRIDAY

SUBJECT	MON	TUES	WED	THUR	FRIDAY

SUBJECT	MON	TUES	WED	THUR	FRIDAY

SUBJECT	MON	TUES	WED	THUR	FRIDAY

SUBJECT	MON	TUES	WED	THUR	FRIDAY

SUBJECT	MON	TUES	WED	THUR	FRIDAY

Weekly ASSIGNMENTS

WEEK OF _____

✓
COMPLETED

- ○ _____
- ○ _____
- ○ _____
- ○ _____
- ○ _____
- ○ _____
- ○ _____
- ○ _____
- ○ _____
- ○ _____

Videos WATCHED

NAME OF MOVIE/VIDEO

_____

_____

_____

_____

_____

_____

_____

NOTES

Monthly RECAP

Stop stressing about...

Ideas

Conversations

Things to do

Shopping list

-
-
-
-
-
-
-
-
-

Explore and learn about...

JUNE

Sunday	Monday	Tuesday	Wednesday
		1	2
6	7	8	9
13	14	15	16
20 Father's Day	21	22	23
27	28	29	30

2021

Thursday	Friday	Saturday
3	4 National Donut Day	5
10	11	12
17	18	19
24	25	26

183

S	M	T	W	T	F	S
						1
2	3	4	5	6	7	8
9	10	11	12	13	14	15
16	17	18	19	20	21	22
23	24	25	26	27	28	29
30	31					

LIST

○ _____

○ _____

○ _____

○ _____

○ _____

○ _____

○ _____

○ _____

○ _____

○ _____

○ _____

JULY 2021

S	M	T	W	T	F	S
				1	2	3
4	5	6	7	8	9	10
11	12	13	14	15	16	17
18	19	20	21	22	23	24
25	26	27	28	29	30	31

MONTHLY *Reading Register*

BOOK TITLE	DATE FINISHED

Reading Wish List

Weekly Plan

WEEK OF

TO DO'S/ *Notes*

_____
_____
_____
_____
_____
_____
_____
_____
_____
_____
_____
_____
_____
_____
_____
_____
_____
_____
_____
_____
_____
_____
_____

Goals

Projects

185

Weekly Curriculum Plan

WEEK OF

SUBJECT	MON	TUES	WED	THUR	FRIDAY

SUBJECT	MON	TUES	WED	THUR	FRIDAY

SUBJECT	MON	TUES	WED	THUR	FRIDAY

SUBJECT	MON	TUES	WED	THUR	FRIDAY

SUBJECT	MON	TUES	WED	THUR	FRIDAY

SUBJECT	MON	TUES	WED	THUR	FRIDAY

Weekly ASSIGNMENTS

WEEK OF _____

✓
COMPLETED

- ○ _____
- ○ _____
- ○ _____
- ○ _____
- ○ _____
- ○ _____
- ○ _____
- ○ _____
- ○ _____
- ○ _____

Videos WATCHED

NAME OF MOVIE/VIDEO

_____
_____
_____
_____
_____
_____

NOTES

Weekly Plan

TO DO'S/ *Notes*

Goals

Projects

188

Weekly Curriculum Plan

WEEK OF

SUBJECT	MON	TUES	WED	THUR	FRIDAY

SUBJECT	MON	TUES	WED	THUR	FRIDAY

SUBJECT	MON	TUES	WED	THUR	FRIDAY

SUBJECT	MON	TUES	WED	THUR	FRIDAY

SUBJECT	MON	TUES	WED	THUR	FRIDAY

SUBJECT	MON	TUES	WED	THUR	FRIDAY

Weekly ASSIGNMENTS

WEEK OF

✓
COMPLETED

- ○
- ○
- ○
- ○
- ○
- ○
- ○
- ○
- ○
- ○

Videos WATCHED

NAME OF MOVIE/VIDEO

NOTES

Weekly Plan

TO DO'S/ *Notes*

Goals

Projects

191

Weekly Curriculum Plan

SUBJECT	MON	TUES	WED	THUR	FRIDAY

SUBJECT	MON	TUES	WED	THUR	FRIDAY

SUBJECT	MON	TUES	WED	THUR	FRIDAY

SUBJECT	MON	TUES	WED	THUR	FRIDAY

SUBJECT	MON	TUES	WED	THUR	FRIDAY

SUBJECT	MON	TUES	WED	THUR	FRIDAY

Weekly ASSIGNMENTS

WEEK OF _____

✓ COMPLETED

- ○
- ○
- ○
- ○
- ○
- ○
- ○
- ○
- ○
- ○

Videos WATCHED

NAME OF MOVIE/VIDEO

NOTES

Weekly Plan

TO DO'S/ *Notes*

_____
_____
_____
_____
_____
_____
_____
_____
_____
_____
_____
_____
_____
_____
_____
_____
_____
_____
_____
_____
_____
_____
_____
_____

Goals

Projects

Weekly Curriculum Plan

WEEK OF

SUBJECT	MON	TUES	WED	THUR	FRIDAY

SUBJECT	MON	TUES	WED	THUR	FRIDAY

SUBJECT	MON	TUES	WED	THUR	FRIDAY

SUBJECT	MON	TUES	WED	THUR	FRIDAY

SUBJECT	MON	TUES	WED	THUR	FRIDAY

SUBJECT	MON	TUES	WED	THUR	FRIDAY

Weekly ASSIGNMENTS

WEEK OF

✓
COMPLETED

○ _____
○ _____
○ _____
○ _____
○ _____
○ _____
○ _____
○ _____
○ _____
○ _____

Videos WATCHED

NAME OF MOVIE/VIDEO

_____
_____
_____
_____
_____
_____

NOTES

Monthly RECAP

Stop stressing about...

Ideas

Conversations

Shopping list

- •
- •
- •
- •
- •
- •
- •
- •
- •

Things to do

Explore and learn about...

JULY

Sunday	Monday	Tuesday	Wednesday
4 Independence Day	5	6	7
11	12	13	14
18	19	20	21
25 Parent's Day	26	27	28

2021

Thursday	Friday	Saturday
1	2	3
8	9	10
15	16	17
22	23	24
29	30	31

JUNE 2021

S	M	T	W	T	F	S
		1	2	3	4	5
6	7	8	9	10	11	12
13	14	15	16	17	18	19
20	21	22	23	24	25	26
27	28	29	30			

LIST

- ○ _____
- ○ _____
- ○ _____
- ○ _____
- ○ _____
- ○ _____
- ○ _____
- ○ _____
- ○ _____
- ○ _____
- ○ _____

AUGUST 2021

S	M	T	W	T	F	S
1	2	3	4	5	6	7
8	9	10	11	12	13	14
15	16	17	18	19	20	21
22	23	24	25	26	27	28
29	30	31				

MONTHLY *Reading Register*

BOOK TITLE	DATE FINISHED

Reading Wish List

Weekly Plan

TO DO'S/ *Notes*

_____
_____
_____
_____
_____
_____
_____
_____
_____
_____
_____
_____
_____
_____
_____
_____
_____
_____
_____
_____
_____
_____
_____

Goals

Projects

201

Weekly Curriculum Plan

WEEK OF

SUBJECT	MON	TUES	WED	THUR	FRIDAY

SUBJECT	MON	TUES	WED	THUR	FRIDAY

SUBJECT	MON	TUES	WED	THUR	FRIDAY

SUBJECT	MON	TUES	WED	THUR	FRIDAY

SUBJECT	MON	TUES	WED	THUR	FRIDAY

SUBJECT	MON	TUES	WED	THUR	FRIDAY

Weekly ASSIGNMENTS

WEEK OF

✓
COMPLETED

- ○
- ○
- ○
- ○
- ○
- ○
- ○
- ○
- ○
- ○

Videos WATCHED

NAME OF MOVIE/VIDEO

NOTES

Weekly Plan

TO DO'S/ *Notes*

Goals

Projects

Weekly Curriculum Plan

WEEK OF

SUBJECT	MON	TUES	WED	THUR	FRIDAY

SUBJECT	MON	TUES	WED	THUR	FRIDAY

SUBJECT	MON	TUES	WED	THUR	FRIDAY

SUBJECT	MON	TUES	WED	THUR	FRIDAY

SUBJECT	MON	TUES	WED	THUR	FRIDAY

SUBJECT	MON	TUES	WED	THUR	FRIDAY

Weekly ASSIGNMENTS

WEEK OF

✓
COMPLETED

- ○
- ○
- ○
- ○
- ○
- ○
- ○
- ○
- ○
- ○

Videos WATCHED

NAME OF MOVIE/VIDEO

NOTES

Weekly Plan

TO DO'S/ *Notes*

_____
_____
_____
_____
_____
_____
_____
_____
_____
_____
_____
_____
_____
_____
_____
_____
_____
_____
_____
_____
_____
_____
_____
_____
_____

Goals

Projects

Weekly Curriculum Plan

WEEK OF

SUBJECT	MON	TUES	WED	THUR	FRIDAY

SUBJECT	MON	TUES	WED	THUR	FRIDAY

SUBJECT	MON	TUES	WED	THUR	FRIDAY

SUBJECT	MON	TUES	WED	THUR	FRIDAY

SUBJECT	MON	TUES	WED	THUR	FRIDAY

SUBJECT	MON	TUES	WED	THUR	FRIDAY

Weekly ASSIGNMENTS

WEEK OF _____

✓
COMPLETED

- ○
- ○
- ○
- ○
- ○
- ○
- ○
- ○
- ○
- ○

Videos WATCHED

NAME OF MOVIE/VIDEO

_____

_____

_____

_____

_____

_____

NOTES

Weekly Plan

TO DO'S/ *Notes*

_____
_____
_____
_____
_____
_____
_____
_____
_____
_____
_____
_____
_____
_____
_____
_____
_____
_____
_____
_____
_____
_____
_____
_____

Goals

Projects

210

Weekly Curriculum Plan

WEEK OF

SUBJECT	MON	TUES	WED	THUR	FRIDAY

SUBJECT	MON	TUES	WED	THUR	FRIDAY

SUBJECT	MON	TUES	WED	THUR	FRIDAY

SUBJECT	MON	TUES	WED	THUR	FRIDAY

SUBJECT	MON	TUES	WED	THUR	FRIDAY

SUBJECT	MON	TUES	WED	THUR	FRIDAY

Weekly ASSIGNMENTS

WEEK OF

✓ COMPLETED

- ○
- ○
- ○
- ○
- ○
- ○
- ○
- ○
- ○
- ○

Videos WATCHED

NAME OF MOVIE/VIDEO

NOTES

Monthly RECAP

Stop stressing about...

Ideas

Conversations

Shopping list

-
-
-
-
-
-
-
-
-

Things to do

Explore and learn about...

AUGUST

Sunday	Monday	Tuesday	Wednesday
1	2	3	4
8	9	10	11
15	16	17	18
22	23	24	25
29	30	31	

2021

Thursday	Friday	Saturday
5	6	7
12	13	14
19 National Aviation Day	20	21
26	27	28

JULY 2021

S	M	T	W	T	F	S
				1	2	3
4	5	6	7	8	9	10
11	12	13	14	15	16	17
18	19	20	21	22	23	24
25	26	27	28	29	30	31

LIST

○ _____

○ _____

○ _____

○ _____

○ _____

○ _____

○ _____

○ _____

○ _____

○ _____

○ _____

SEPTEMBER 2021

S	M	T	W	T	F	S
			1	2	3	4
5	6	7	8	9	10	11
12	13	14	15	16	17	18
19	20	21	22	23	24	25
26	27	28	29	30		

MONTHLY *Reading Register*

BOOK TITLE	DATE FINISHED

Reading Wish List

_____

_____

_____

_____

Weekly Plan

TO DO'S/ *Notes*

Goals

Projects

217

Weekly Curriculum Plan

WEEK OF

SUBJECT	MON	TUES	WED	THUR	FRIDAY

SUBJECT	MON	TUES	WED	THUR	FRIDAY

SUBJECT	MON	TUES	WED	THUR	FRIDAY

SUBJECT	MON	TUES	WED	THUR	FRIDAY

SUBJECT	MON	TUES	WED	THUR	FRIDAY

SUBJECT	MON	TUES	WED	THUR	FRIDAY

Weekly ASSIGNMENTS

WEEK OF

✓
COMPLETED

- ○
- ○
- ○
- ○
- ○
- ○
- ○
- ○
- ○
- ○

Videos WATCHED

NAME OF MOVIE/VIDEO

NOTES

Weekly Plan

TO DO'S/ *Notes*

_____
_____
_____
_____
_____
_____
_____
_____
_____
_____
_____
_____
_____
_____
_____
_____
_____
_____
_____
_____
_____
_____
_____
_____

Goals

Projects

220

Weekly Curriculum Plan

WEEK OF

SUBJECT	MON	TUES	WED	THUR	FRIDAY

SUBJECT	MON	TUES	WED	THUR	FRIDAY

SUBJECT	MON	TUES	WED	THUR	FRIDAY

SUBJECT	MON	TUES	WED	THUR	FRIDAY

SUBJECT	MON	TUES	WED	THUR	FRIDAY

SUBJECT	MON	TUES	WED	THUR	FRIDAY

Weekly ASSIGNMENTS

WEEK OF _____

✓
COMPLETED

- ○ _____
- ○ _____
- ○ _____
- ○ _____
- ○ _____
- ○ _____
- ○ _____
- ○ _____
- ○ _____
- ○ _____

Videos WATCHED

NAME OF MOVIE/VIDEO

_____

_____

_____

_____

_____

_____

NOTES

Weekly Plan

TO DO'S/ *Notes*

_____
_____
_____
_____
_____
_____
_____
_____
_____
_____
_____
_____
_____
_____
_____
_____
_____
_____
_____
_____
_____
_____
_____

Goals

Projects

223

Weekly Curriculum Plan

WEEK OF

SUBJECT	MON	TUES	WED	THUR	FRIDAY

SUBJECT	MON	TUES	WED	THUR	FRIDAY

SUBJECT	MON	TUES	WED	THUR	FRIDAY

SUBJECT	MON	TUES	WED	THUR	FRIDAY

SUBJECT	MON	TUES	WED	THUR	FRIDAY

SUBJECT	MON	TUES	WED	THUR	FRIDAY

Weekly ASSIGNMENTS

WEEK OF _____

✓
COMPLETED

- ○
- ○
- ○
- ○
- ○
- ○
- ○
- ○
- ○
- ○

Videos WATCHED

NAME OF MOVIE/VIDEO

NOTES

Weekly Plan

TO DO'S/ *Notes*

_____
_____
_____
_____
_____
_____
_____
_____
_____
_____
_____
_____
_____
_____
_____
_____
_____
_____
_____
_____
_____
_____
_____
_____

Goals

Projects

Weekly Curriculum Plan

WEEK OF

SUBJECT	MON	TUES	WED	THUR	FRIDAY

SUBJECT	MON	TUES	WED	THUR	FRIDAY

SUBJECT	MON	TUES	WED	THUR	FRIDAY

SUBJECT	MON	TUES	WED	THUR	FRIDAY

SUBJECT	MON	TUES	WED	THUR	FRIDAY

SUBJECT	MON	TUES	WED	THUR	FRIDAY

Weekly ASSIGNMENTS

WEEK OF

✓
COMPLETED

- ○
- ○
- ○
- ○
- ○
- ○
- ○
- ○
- ○
- ○

Videos WATCHED

NAME OF MOVIE/VIDEO

NOTES

Monthly RECAP

Stop stressing about...

Ideas

Conversations

Shopping list

-
-
-
-
-
-
-
-
-

Things to do

Explore and learn about...

GRADE REGISTER | *Semester 2*

SUBJECT: _____

Date	Assignment or Test	Points Possible	Points Achieved	Grade
	Semester 2 Grade			

SUBJECT: _____

Date	Assignment or Test	Points Possible	Points Achieved	Grade
	Semester 2 Grade			

GRADE REGISTER | Semester 2

SUBJECT: _____

Date	Assignment or Test	Points Possible	Points Achieved	Grade
		Semester 2 Grade		

SUBJECT: _____

Date	Assignment or Test	Points Possible	Points Achieved	Grade
		Semester 2 Grade		

GRADE REGISTER | *Semester 2*

SUBJECT: _____

Date	Assignment or Test	Points Possible	Points Achieved	Grade
		Semester 2 Grade		

SUBJECT: _____

Date	Assignment or Test	Points Possible	Points Achieved	Grade
		Semester 2 Grade		

GRADE REGISTER | *Semester 2*

SUBJECT: _____

Date	Assignment or Test	Points Possible	Points Achieved	Grade
Semester 2 Grade				

SUBJECT: _____

Date	Assignment or Test	Points Possible	Points Achieved	Grade
Semester 2 Grade				

YEAR END *Student Reflections*

SUCCESSES:

_____

_____

_____

_____

HABITS:

_____

_____

_____

_____

CHARACTER:

_____

_____

_____

_____

WHAT CAN WE DO BETTER?

_____

_____

_____

_____

OTHER NOTES:

_____

_____

_____

Notes

Notes

Next Year At A Glance

NOTES:

- _____

AUGUST

_____

- _____

SEPTEMBER

_____

- _____

OCTOBER

_____

- _____

NOVEMBER

_____

- _____

DECEMBER

_____

- _____

JANUARY

_____

GOAL

OF WEEKS _____

OF DAYS _____

Next Year At A Glance

NOTES:

FEBRUARY

- _____

MARCH

- _____

APRIL

- _____

MAY

- _____

JUNE

- _____

JULY

- _____

GOAL

OF WEEKS _____

OF DAYS _____

Ideas for Next Year

Ideas for Next Year